DISCARD

Happy Hour

Phoenix Poets
A Series Edited by Robert von Hallberg

Happy Hour
Alan Shapiro

The University of Chicago Press
Chicago and London

ALAN SHAPIRO, associate professor of English at Northwestern University, has been awarded fellowships by the National Endowment for the Arts and the John Simon Guggenheim Memorial Foundation. He is the author of two previous volumes of poetry, *After the Digging* and, also in the Phoenix Poets series, *The Courtesy*.

The University of Chicago Press, Chicago 60637
The University of Chicago Press, Ltd., London

© 1987 by The University of Chicago
All rights reserved. Published 1987
Printed in the United States of America
96 95 94 93 92 91 90 89 88 87   54321

Library of Congress Cataloging-in-Publication Data

Shapiro, Alan, 1952–
  Happy hour.

  (Phoenix poets)
  I. Title. II. Series.
PS3569.H338H3 1987   811'.54   86-11279
ISBN 0-226-75028-0
ISBN 0-226-75029-9 (pbk.)

Grateful acknowledgment is made to the following magazines and journals for publishing these poems and for allowing them to be reprinted:

American Scholar: "Homage"
Crazyhorse: "Other Hands," "A Christmas Story"
Denver Quarterly: "Walkman," Blue Vase," "Neighbors"
The New Criterion: "Familiar Story," "Vine"
The New Republic: "Astronomy Lesson"
Southwest Review: "Lace Fern," "Otter Island"
Threepenny Review: "The Riddle"
TriQuarterly: "Happy Hour," "Genie," "Bedtime Story," "Extra"

Thanks also go to the National Endowment for the Arts for a fellowship that supported the completion of this book.

We cannot speak a loyal word and be meanly silent, we cannot kill and not kill in the same moment; but a moment is room wide enough for the loyal and mean desires, for the outlash of a murderous thought and the sharp backward stroke of repentance.

—George Eliot, *Daniel Deronda*

And hearths, extinguished, cast a gloom for miles.
—Donald Davie, "Homage to William Cowper"

Contents

Happy Hour

The gregarious dark is shifting
when she puts her second drink,
the free one, half on the coaster.
The tipped wine poised at the brim
is the beginning of the bad girl
she'll promise never to be again
tomorrow, who can taunt him now
to prove he doesn't love her
and never could: her hand slides
up his thigh until he tenses—
"My little prig, don't you want
to fuck me?," the bad girl
she couldn't be at home, his wife on ice.
All he can do is smile back
as though she's made a harmless
good-natured joke, and struggle
not to look around to see
who's heard, who's watching. He wants
to smash the wine glass in her face
so he can know for once
exactly what he's done wrong;
but he places it instead
back safely on the coaster
quickly before she sees.
Never cautious enough, he is prepared
even if she knocks it over
to go down on his hands and knees
and wipe it up, kind and forgiving.
In all ways careful to acquit himself
so that tomorrow when she says
she doesn't deserve him, he's too good,
he can believe her. Tomorrow
will be *his* happy hour. There won't be
anything she wouldn't do for him.

1

Genie

Though he would drink with her, he never drank as much
as fast, and often early on those evenings
she'd sense his stiff refusal as the gin fell.
Well, both had their parts, and needed them.
Honoring that need, she'd hurry along their words
from scene to scene, each more furious with meaning:
Neglected Wife and Disappointed Husband, the faithfully
directed tit-for-tats that always ended
with his back blurred in the glass as he'd dissolve to bed;
herself, at last, abandoned to her favorite role,
a genie in reverse: now she'd slip cleanly
into the snug hold of another bottle
where she was rid of him, so she could grant him
what she knew must be his secret wish.

Walkman

"Sure, I'm a fat bitch!
What of it?" The voice shrill,
jittery, in the fog
somewhere to his right,
slowing his step—"What
of it?" to a husband, or
to no one, maybe to him
though he keeps walking,
doesn't pause or look. Fog
everywhere around him,
it seems, but where he is.
It supples the sweatsuit
jogging toward him to a smoky
whiteness every stride
is brightening, each footstep
glum on the wet leaves.
The same fog as a child
he would dream of hovering in
above his own grave, looking
down on the thick ring
of family and friends and teachers—
delighted by the serious grief,
their remorse for all the slights
and punishments they would do
anything to undo now.
Now no slammed doors,
no words. Only the provocations
he goes over and over
on his long walks, and the invoice
of anger he never shows . . .
In the empty artificial pond
someone is roller skating
across the sunken bottom.
A Walkman clipped to his belt,

in headphones, dark
shades, hands on hips,
he figure-eights from one
end to the other, skating
backward now, and forward,
to music no one else can hear,
that each quick pirouette and
sliding stride's the fluent
motion of. So beautiful
it almost seems he wishes
he were someone else
so he could watch himself
each time he disappears
in fog, and reappears—
so he could see each time
for the first time just how
flawless he can be, his dark
shades saying how untouchable.

Homage

Especially on those nights
when both of them keep fighting
and they fall asleep still mad,
he wakes hearing the pigeons
high up inside the chimney
fluttering down, settling.
Almost like lovers, the way
all rustle close together,
shift to give each other room;
cooing so briefly, faintly,
as though they each have wakened
only enough to know that
they are sleeping now, and warm.
And he draws up close to her,
his chest full against her back,
her hand in his. He's thinking
it would almost be a kind
of homage to their old love
to fall back asleep before
recalling that it's really
only anybody's warmth
now, which they receive and give.

Lace Fern

1

Like a word we need to say
to remember, the lace fern
on the sill stirs suddenly:
Now thin stem and sloping frond,
spine more hair than spine, more mist
than hair, dwell in a brightening
turn toward the arriving light.

2

Unaware of having wakened me,
you were humming to yourself before the mirror.
So I kept quiet; in our bed behind you
glad to be awake without your knowing,
I watched as you drew the brush down
through the loose braids your other hand was holding,
tilting your head a little, your back arched.
And I began to think that your long hair
brightening where the brush would pass
became the furthest edge of what you hummed,
yourself hardly in the room. That tune,
makeshift and cracked, was anything but beautiful,
yet it seemed to lead you off, as if it came
from another room, and was beautiful only there.
So deeply had you gone into that spacious humming
I couldn't tell if it was brush or hand
absently drawing the other
through the braids now blurred into a single tress.
Even later I was afraid to say
how I stayed quiet and, happy for your sake,
kept to myself the unsuspected
secret you confided.

3

Outside, as you crossed the window
you paused, opening your bag
to make sure you had everything.
For a moment the fern held you,
your hair woven into the fine
green netting, shining
in the same light. And when you left
the fern shaped what was past
into a tracery
of small innumerable spaces
only the light can fill.

Scattered Places

Up and down the creek, maple and giant beech
and, under them, the darker sloping hemlock
fold shadow onto shadow to the water's edge.
Sunlight only in scattered places
sprouting between leaves, from other leaves,
flaring from wet stones. On higher ground
my lovers turn with the creek, and disappear.
I've stayed behind to look for arrowhead or shard,
the wake on stone of wing tip, fin or leaf.
But I found nothing. So now I turn back toward them
slowly wading through steep grass and briar
along the bank, watching for loose stones,
dead trees soft as moss, half-melted into fern.
Quietly, quietly, stone and branch and small fish
hang in the current. The water threshes what it holds.
And when the creek turns, I still can't see them.
Their names go, wakeless, through the air.

Familiar Story

Tonight they need to be both host and stranger,
talking together all evening after dinner;
the candle wavering down till they are half
in darkness as they lead each other back
through their accumulated separate lore,
telling the stories they have told before
to other lovers, who are stories now.
They give no truth here, but the practised glow
of truthfulness: even as they confess
wholeheartedly to niggling attentiveness
disguised as love, to no or too much care,
affection parceled out till it's not there—
the more one tells, the more the other sees
just how appealing is this honesty,
how generous they are to those who hurt them.
They think this kind shrewd vision won't desert them.
And tonight, at least, it won't as they forget
what all their lore will lead them to expect
of one another, what they'll later owe
day after each slow day when all they know
is the familiar story they are living,
restless, and remote, and unforgiving.
It's then, when they don't feel it, they will need
the love bad days require and impede.
But not tonight, the candle going, gone,
their eyes shut briefly as the light goes on.
Tonight desire is generosity,
desire in each other's all they see,
and all else now is no more than the light
hurting their eyes, too sudden and too bright.

Vine
for Della

The previous tenants must have left it here
because it settled twisting up around
the trellis of the mullioned windows so
tenaciously they couldn't take it down;

they couldn't budge the huge pot on the floor
for all the tendrils rooted in the cracks
between the window and the window frame,
pressing their heart-shaped leaves against the glass.

So we could trace out every kind of weather:
a cross unyielding sun in the burned tips,
or shade no sun could break where deep green paled
and narrowed in a whitening eclipse.

Or days, like this day, when the early light
brings all out of doors into the waiting leaves
which suddenly have known no other time
than dwelling in this green light light receives.

Blue Vase

Now and again, I look up as I clean,
and the large room we quarreled over,
arranging and rearranging it all week,
surprises me this morning, stiller somehow
for the tangled shadowy commotion light
is making on the freshly painted walls
and varnished floors, around you working there
bent over at the table. Slowly you run
the hem of what will be our bedroom curtains
under the needle pumping faster now,
now slower, blurring and coming into view.
I think my things begin to seem less shy
here next to yours: our couches at an angle,
quilted with shadows which the sunlight weaves
and unweaves all day long, day after day;
your oak chest in between them, and on the chest
a lamp and small blue vase my ex-wife left
behind so many months ago. Blue vase,
and lamp, and couch, the table where you sew—
suddenly for the first time they remind me
not so insistently of my old place,
the other rooms in which I once arranged them
as carefully as we have now, as though for good.
Suddenly for the first time I can imagine
being years from my last thought of her,
that past life, old intimacies, the small talk—
tender or quarrelsome—our days and nights
unfolded in those rooms only, nowhere else.

Even if months from now some small detail
should come to mind, hearing myself say something
she would say, her voice entangled with
my voice a moment, I know now it will come
only to prove how easily I had
forgotten it till then, how easily

it is relinquished. I dust the blue vase off.
I buff it to a stringent sheen.
How odd that I should have to tell myself,
today, I was at home there all those years,
woven into that intricate design
so deeply, sadly, certain it was durable
if only because it seemed to fray so long.
And though a long time after I would struggle
to believe it was my leaving, not living there,
that made those rooms seem magical, today
it's the belief itself that saddens me:
it comes so easily. What saddens me today
is that I'm home.
                              You call me over.
You're smiling because the curtains in your hands—
white curtains with blue flowers and yellow flowers—
fall everywhere about you, fold on fold,
as you try to hold them up. And I smile too,
taking the other edge, surprised how much
I have to lean back, one knee bent, to keep
that plentiful bright cloth above the floor
it grazes now, no matter what I do.

Neighbors

1

Not that the neighborhood was bad,
he explained from the station wagon
already idling, packed full of boxes,
suitcases, and a large yucca lolling
like a tongue out of the back hatch—
no, there were more locks on the doors
than ribbons on a general because,
well, you know, he was a cop and
had a family to think of. Yes,
of course, we understood, somehow
not quite relieved. "Your downstairs
neighbor," he said too casually
as he handed us the keys and gestured
to the nightgowned woman
filling the sun porch window:

She was all torsion, swaying backward
and forward to the dull bass
thumping behind her as she sang
into the absent microphone
she held in one hand, the other raking
her lank hair, "If you'll hold
the ladder, baby, I'll climb to the top."

"I know what you're thinking. I know.
But she's not so bad. Really. Enjoy."
And the hatch flapped up and down
over the yucca, laughing, laughing
down the street straight for the suburbs.

2

Only after we had scrubbed the shadow
of other pictures from the walls
and painted and hung our own
up in different places, knocked down
the wall between the sun porch
and dining room, and in the new light
flooding the now larger rooms
no sign remained that anyone
but us had ever lived there.
Only then, the whole place poised
with our future, the rooms
themselves a glistening array
of days this new arrangement of our things
would conjure. Only then we noticed
that the stereo downstairs was playing,
had been playing all week as we worked,
the same bass trembling in the floor,
the same bent twang of phrases we
could make out now and again
and all that night, Climb to the top,
the ladder, baby, baby, climb to the top.

3

Three days of banging on the door
she wouldn't open, the song
louder, each time we shouted
turn it down. Then this:
"Dear Neighbors: I am sorry
if my music bothers you.
Since the police never minded
I did not think I was breaking
any laws. Could you please
stop banging on my door.
I am doing research in
natural healing. I am trying
to cure a paralyzed kid
with music, and the banging
is very bad for all of us
down here. If my research
continues to disturb you
I will find another place
to do it. Yours, your Neighbor."

4

He broke her favorite cup.
It slipped from his soapy fingers
against the sink and split
down the belly of the brown deer
leaping stiffly for the leaves
up at the rim. "It's nothing,"
she assured him, "don't worry."
Yet the more he asked her
what was wrong, the more
that he wouldn't stop
asking her became the trouble.
All evening, the covers drawn up
tight around her, she read,
she tried to read. She tried
not to think about the years
the cup was hers before she knew him,
the other men who had loved her,
his other women, more vivid now,
more intimate, for being past.
She tried not to hear the song
downstairs that drifted through the bedroom,
the lush pleading of that relentless
lover as they lay side by side,
awake, in the cool sheets—
Oh babe, Oh honey-child of mine,
My one desire, as though
to ask her, was there anyone
who ever loved like this?

5

Her back is shadow, her other side all light.
For a moment he can watch her in the glazed lamp,
the loosened watery shining of her neck and shoulder,
the full slope of her breast, and down, to the rough
hint of her hip where the sheet has paused. He notices
how bright his hand turns crossing her side to take
the book still cupped in her palm. Afraid to wake her,
and wanting to, as gently as he can
he lets the sheet slip down a little further
as he reaches up and switches off the lamp.

6

We began to think she must have
known that we were listening,
by then, whenever the song ended,
that we had to stop talking
or look up from the paper
we couldn't keep from rustling,
trying each time to be as quiet
as the quiet she controlled.
Yes, we were sure she held
the arm of the stereo above
the spinning 45, and waited,
knowing we were so alert
with waiting that we could almost
hear, and wanted to hear by then
the needle sink to the smooth
thin band and slide across it
and catch in the first groove,
so we could go on talking,
go on reading the paper, go
on doing whatever it was, by then,
she was allowing us to do.

7

As he typed the note the landlord
had dictated over the phone

"Mr. Sheldon Pearle of Pearle
and Pernish Realtors has been
calling you all weekend.
This message is being sent
at great expense by a special
messenger"

                    he didn't need
to remind himself about the fate
of messengers, and was grateful
this time for the eternal
I can't live without you
whining which concealed him
as he slipped the note in
under her door and left

"He has received reports
you are at home because
the stereo is playing.
If you do not return
his call, a lawsuit will
be instigated forthwith"

only to discover
that her phone was ringing
in time to the song
it was his fate to struggle
not to hear or hum.

8

Because they were outside
in front of the building
and he was afraid, as always,

that someone would see them kissing,
his kiss was quick, efficient, a
furtive dispatch of her that

made her feel as he drove off
that they were someone else's wife
and husband, cheating on themselves.

"Nice," she said, "that's nice,"
the woman in the window smiling,
her nightgown like trampled snow.

"My man is coming soon and the
four of us should get together."
The voice too girlish—to mock her?

she wondered as she hurried
upstairs and locked all the locks,
leaning her whole weight against them.

Yes, he'd come soon, and their messy
opulent displays would be there
in the window for all to see.

That man would come while upstairs
she and hers worked harder on the busy
reciprocities, the tidy

quid pro quo concerns that
made them the nice people no one
would look twice at on the street.

9

Each touch a gratitude of touching,
a sleight of hand in which desires
he's too abashed, or proud,
to tell yet still resents her
afterward for not divining
vanish in the unbiddable,
unanticipated turns and slow
prolongings of their pleasure,
the resinous sweet salt
signature of it on belly,
thigh and lip . . .
                    A paper airplane
on the walk next morning stops him.
The nose crumpled, wings uneven,
gawky, so that it must have made
a drunken beeline for the concrete
swirling straight down when she let it go.
On both sides of it a large scrawl,
the letters wobbly as though they strained
against some indecipherable agitation:
"Dear President Marcos, May God grant
all Oriental people peace. May God grant
all Oriental people health and prosperity.
May God grant all Oriental people shelter . . ."
And on and on, the letters larger,
wilder, spasming down the page till
by the end they seem like letters
only by accident—"May God grant
all Oriental people loose shoes, a warm
place to shit, clean sheets, good fucking."

So many blondes and brunettes and redheads
leaning toward him as he sits in traffic—
they smile down from the billboards

bright with whiskey, health spas,
cigarettes—their serious breasts,
brushed tans and sidelong glances,
cunning with consent, are gorgeous blanks
desire fills in only as it will.
At each red light the women
he has to notice as they saunter
by before him (not even pretty,
just unknown, not his) are shills
employed, he thinks, by this content-less
longing after more and better,
bumper to bumper, on his way to work.

Last night so remote already, the memory
a small port growing smaller in the swell
of expectations—saviour, stud,
whore, counselor—already crowding
his day and hers. Capricious pleasure,
frail craft, how long, he wonders,
how far will it carry them?
How good does it need to be?

10

The middle of May, and she orders
firewood. Whenever we came in
or out that day we saw her
in the hot glass, her eyes fixed
on the logs dumped in the front yard.
Like a ventriloquist, she hardly moved
her lips to the song behind her
that was louder now, turned up
against the phone that rang
and rang.
                    Past midnight
wood clattered on the walk.
She was out there, frantic, lugging
log after log into the building.
"Get away from me," she yelled
when I went down to help,
"I know you, get away."
                              Two weeks later
the police broke down her door
and the thick charred stench
from the fire she had blazing
night and day rose up the stairwell
where we watched her, handcuffed,
being led away, mumbling the song.
Someone (not us) had called them.
Yet in the sudden quiet
we could not get used to
we couldn't help but think back
to the night she lugged the wood in,
the way she wildly looked around
when the car lights slashed across
her chafed arms, her wet nightgown,
her suffering unhoused, exposed

to anybody's eyes. And we thought about
our urge to go on watching.

What did she feel then, the wood
all safe, and the fire catching?
Was it the way we pictured it?
The way, now, we wanted it to be?
Did she draw the curtains, tell
herself it would be hours yet
before the phone would ring—
at ease, at last, because the song
was playing, and her man, her one
desire, was climbing up the blazing
ladder no one else could see?

The Riddle

Long ago, a little boy is winding up his soldier,
his concentration as deep as instinct as he turns
the brass key on the soldier's back easily at first,

then slowly, slower, twisting the key as far as it will go.
His mother at the stove in front of him is stirring
the huge pot steaming up into her face, and saying

over and over that he's a bad boy, a heart attack
he'll give her, is that what he wants? will that
make him happy? He is like the blue flames

under the pot, blue stars she makes appear
and disappear. He grips the key hard to keep himself
from going where her voice would send him,

his fingers reddening against it, beginning to tremble
as the coiled spring grows more eager, more insistent.
But he holds on, grips it harder; he's waiting

till he feels the poised soldier and his fingers merge
into a single yearning he can't hold back any longer,
till he needs to pull his hand away so badly

that it nearly feels like a bad thing to do.
The spring coils through him, knots and goes on knotting:
was it the blue flame he was reaching out to touch

that burned him then, or her hard hand slapping his?
The fire in her voice and on his hand all twisted now
as far as they will go, a riddle he can't solve

except to jerk his hand away as from another fire.
The key whirrs so furiously it disappears.
The soldier charges across the table toward his mother

and is just about to shoot her dead when he plunges
over the table's edge down to the floor
where the boy retrieves him, winds him up again,

grips him so his fingers burn, so the soldier can run
again like punishment against her, and again be punished
over and over for the bad thing he is about to do.

26

Bedtime Story

When his mother ends each story
the child can hear a bad wind
break through the elms. It makes him think
the trees, torn up, are going.
Hansel and Gretel, Three Little Pigs—
he wants to crawl up inside them, he wants
to be tucked safely in his mother's voice
so he can't hear the window
shaking, or that new man
calling her name out from the other room.

But his mother says, this is the last time,
and reads so impatiently, her voice
already leaving, that the bad wind
carries away the boy and girl
and the three pigs, leaving the child—
when the light goes off—
awake inside another
story, where the witch revives
and the wolf blows down the walls.

Other Hands

When the rabbit crouched down
and shivered, hiding within itself,
our teacher said the person
it came to could care for it
the whole day, and no one else.
I couldn't imagine harming it.
I was all wish, like everyone,
and my wish made a secret
passageway for me to cross
to and into it, to its deepest
hiding place where I was whispering
"There, there, you stop crying now,"
the way my mother would when I was
ill or hurt, and the more she whispered
the more I'd have to cry
to keep her whispering,
so I knew why the rabbit still shivered
as my kind voice grew inside it.
And I knew I drew it after me
when I pulled back through the wish
straight past the others till
it crouched down, shivering, in my lap.

The rabbit was never mine enough.
All that day, each time I took it
through the square mesh door
that could have scraped it, or when
I smoothed its long ears back
till its eyes closed to everything
but me, my hands could not stop
whispering on the soft fur, wanting it
to sense through each fretful touch
what harm other hands would do,
what only mine could save it from.

But the next day the rabbit didn't know me.
It nestled in someone else's lap
and the small eyes—shut tight
under another hand—refused to open.
Entirely outside it, I was
nowhere.
      When the others left
my hands turned into other hands—
"Bad boy, you'll learn your lesson"—
scraping the rabbit through the hard door
over and over, for its own good,
so it would not forget.
Even when it broke free
and my stern hands only lowered
like dark clouds against the mesh
the rabbit still crouched down, its head
drawn back in the soft fur
as if to hide, while its shivering repeated
there was now no hiding place,
repeated there was no place now
anywhere inside it that I didn't fill.

Ready or Not

In a corner of the schoolyard, someone's black dog sits
            watching
as a small boy, playing catch against the school, slides dreamily
from side to side over the cracked gravelly blacktop
to scoop the ball up as it rolls back, and throw again, on
and on, so adrowse in unbroken motion it's almost all he is.
The boy can hear the quiet deepening as it closes back like
            water
around the soft thud of the ball, his steady easeful sliding;
he can hear it deepen, even now, around the girl who runs up
singing Puppy! Puppy! to tug at the dog's fur while the dog,
the stillest part of quiet, goes on watching as if she isn't there,
only his dark eyes moving, shimmering dark moons following
            the ball.
The girl's voice and the sleepy drawl of the boy's game cross
and recross like persistent ripples which the quiet smooths
and never quite smooths away.
                              So there's no warning
when a blunt roar breaks the boy's stride and in a deeper quiet
than he's ever heard the girl lies bleeding while the scared dog
looks around as if it wasn't him and might roar back down
            again
from anywhere, at any moment. The schoolyard grows alert
            with it.
It waits where the cracks run through the blacktop; it listens,
an angry wakefulness now everywhere in the air
around the ball the boy throws harder and faster,
needing to see how fast he can make the ball come at him
and still catch it, with the quiet always right there
ready to rush back in around him, around each clean whack
pushing the quiet back till he can feel pain
waking through his arm, till he is ready for it,
till he is only ready, throwing harder, faster.

A Christmas Story

And the Lord said to Moses, "When you go back to Egypt, see
that you do before Pharaoh all the miracles which I have put in
your power; but I will harden his heart, so that he will not let
the people go."
                              Exodus 4:21

It wasn't only envy but also a vague desire
to make amends, to glorify the baby Jesus
with my friend Charlie (who said the Jews had killed him)

that made me sneak into my parent's bedroom
Christmas morning before anyone was awake
to phone Charlie about all the presents

I hadn't received, the tree we didn't have.
Quietly as Santa (whom we must have also killed)
I took the phone down from my father's bedside table

and slipped under the bed into the cramped dark
of springs all intricately crossed and swollen
against me where my father slept. A long time

I lay there cradling the phone; I dialed
when either parent shifted or snored, afraid
that they somehow would answer at the other end;

or hear Charlie's father yelling "Charlie make it quick"
and the forbidden prayer I whispered to him then
of every toy I had ever owned, or seen,

imagining that he imagined all of them right here
under a tree like his, and not the stark menorah,
our stunted version, with its nine thin candles

solemn as school, or the inkstand and underwear—
more chores than gifts—which I received for Chanukah.
No, it was Christmas here under my parent's bed,

it was His manger, and His death was as far from me
as I was from my own house carolling a holy
inventory to my friend. Then he was gone.

The springs became cold law against me as I was hauled
out clinging to the receiver like a hooked fish
to where my father waited, stern as the candles,

fisher of Jews: you want to be a goy, he said,
be a goy, and sent me to my room for the whole day
where it was Chanukah. And I was more a Jew

the more I pictured to myself all of the presents
I had seen at Charlie's house the day before,
a king's treasure, from which the tree ascended

in a pyramid of flames and glittering angels.
On my bare walls, all day, I had to build it
higher and brighter, as though it were a burden

I could not put down, could never escape—
driven to build it all day by a heart
the God of my father, the Lord our God, kept hardening.

Otter Island

Cape Breton, Nova Scotia

The earth was all thick moss between the trees,
giving off a muffled radiance
placeless and unbroken, except for where
the highest leaves rippled the sunlight down
through the watery air. Like greener thicker water
the moss gave way under each cautious step
and made me think, if I stood still long enough,
it would have opened and closed up around me
as it closed around huge stones, or fallen trees,
some now merely places where the moss swelled.

But deeper in, as I turned back clumps of branches
and small sharp leaves, webs breaking against my face,
I found an old trough sunk in tangled vines,
moss covered, like some dream-struggling shape
my scraping would retrieve. How many years?
All I could see was how the metal withered,
cracked where rain water, trickling from higher ground
to break against it, had finally broken through.
Insects tumbled from the dense green fog
into the gash I made, and then ran back

all in a single urge, an ever new
inhabiting . . . Hammer and forge,
shod hoof and path, and the ground cleared—
no greater now than where my fingers scraped.
In that still current, there were no other signs
but the cool sting of leaves against
my arms and wrists, the faintly clinging webs;
what anyone before me had to feel
holding the poised branches back
a moment, where no one had walked for years.

Rickshaw

Outside on the warped card tables all of her old things
seem hardly hers. They're almost new again out here
in this odd light, what she had grown so used to

and stopped seeing, or tired of seeing day after day on
the mantelpiece, coffee table, sill or shelf, and boxed and
        stacked
down in the basement far back in the dark corners, forgotten,

until today. Today they're all glittering with shadows
when the leaves stir. Today she should be happy.
Already she's made fifty, sixty dollars, maybe more,

the loose change in the pocket of her housedress now
so thick it no longer jingles when she moves, heavy
with the promise of what she'll buy. Why does it bother her

to see her neighbors gathered around the tables, chatting
softly as they pick up this electric knife, that necklace,
holding them out to her and asking, Will you take a dollar? . . .

Where in the world did you get this? someone asks,
pointing to an empty rickshaw planter which a little
chinaman is pulling—naked to the waist, and shoeless,

leaning forward with one leg slightly raised, his head bowed
and the wide-brimmed hat pulled down over his face so far
that only the blank line of his mouth is visible.

Where in the world? And suddenly she discovers how little
she can recollect of all the bright occasions—holidays,
or were they shopping sprees?—that carried so many things

year after year into her hands. Now in her neighbors' hands
they remind her of how she wanted them, how they were new
once, so free of her they let her go on wanting

even when they were hers; more promises than things,
glittering totems of their own arrival, they made all life
a present she forever opened until each became,

sooner or later, merely what all life was, a veteran novelty,
the trace of wishes that were vagrant as light,
tireless as the chinaman she takes another dollar for.

She puts her hand into the cool heavy change for
     reassurance—
her shoulders aching with what she's made—and sees a
     neighbor
leave with the rickshaw which the chinaman keeps pulling

out of the yard, across the street, drawing her home
to the mantelpiece, coffee table, sill or shelf where
he can keep on pulling the new plant she will surely buy.

Extra

The heart disease was worth it,
like a gorgeous blouse, expensive
but his favorite color,
like the last word on the subject
they've been arguing for twenty years.
Her friends had told her how
all week he was inconsolable,
how he wasn't sleeping and would cry
the two of them had wasted
all that time not speaking. He swore,
they told her in the private room
he insisted she should have
(though the insurance wouldn't cover it),
somehow he'd make it up to her.
And she answered, good, good.
From now on life would be his
making up to her, wooing her
the way he wooed her all week long,
visiting before work, after work,
each time with flowers, and the nurses
winking, whispering behind his back,
my, my, you have him trained.
For the first time since they moved out here
to start life over, she could think
happily about their new apartment:
the floor to ceiling chinese
lanterns casting an exotic twilight
through the living room, as though
the room were suddenly another
country she was touring through;
and the large white couches and white walls
streaked with a showering fireworks
of thousands of blue and yellow shapes
no two alike, all shimmering

in the glass coffee table
she almost didn't like to use
so it would seem new always,
something no one had ever touched—
it was a Jerusalem of tastefulness,
making their old life back east
a shabby makeshift exile.
But he worried everything, he nagged
dogged as a bill collector:
she was spending too much, why
did they need a decorator, why
an apartment with a pool? His whole life
working himself sick so that he'd have
a little extra for a sick day.

Today, though, as she waited for him
to take her home, she remembered
that the detective show on TV
which shot a scene by their pool
would be on tonight, and they would
watch together. She was an extra.
At the far end of the pool in a lounge chair
she had followed their directions, telling
all about her latest trip
to Acapulco as she murmured
rutabagas, rutabagas, rutabagas
to the woman next to her, who said back
peas and carrots, both of them
almost gawking as the star,
an undercover cop, strolled past them
to the beautiful bikinied girlfriend
of the mob boss he was after.
A woman from his past, she breathes
after the long heartbreaking

look of recognition, "It's
been a long time since El
Paso," and the scene was over.

Back up in the apartment, life
was no longer something that
happened somewhere else, to others.
She was near its rich
stunning heart, she was someone
who belonged, the kind of person
the apartment promised she could be.
But then when he came home and
sat down on his side of the bed,
his back to her, and started
to polish his golf shoes
because, he said, he had an early date
tomorrow on his day off,
and he was beat, and didn't want dinner—
when she stood there, hearing
the lavish wingbeat of the cloth
against the one shoe in his lap,
and staring at the other on the bed
beside him, facing the little
mud streaked spikes, the large
dumb back that never turned,
not even when she walked out,
she realized, she thought for good,
that to tell him anything, anything
at all that had to do with her,
would be to tell him rutabagas,
peas and carrots . . .
                    Yet here he was now
carrying her bags down to the car,
opening the door for her, and asking
almost shyly, like a newlywed,

if she were comfortable, could he do
anything, just name it honey.

Later that day, since he was snoring,
she got up for a cup of coffee.
She was thinking, though the doctors
warned her not to do too much,
that maybe she'd fix him a little
something, when she found a slum
of dishes in the sink, the refrigerator
empty, no coffee, no milk—in the dull
refrigerator glare nothing
had ever seemed so desolate, and yet
fulfilling in a way as she rushed back
breathless, yelling why the hell
hadn't he shopped, or cleaned up?
What was he doing all week?
And he bit back, making a goddamned living.
It was fulfillment of a kind,
the closest she could ever really
get to pleasure, as she got dressed
saying nothing while he stood there,
saying nothing though he followed her
out to the car and pleaded, honey,
make a list and I'll go shopping,
please, honey, let me go . . .

She could still hear him as she drove off.
In the rearview mirror he grew
smaller and smaller, as though seen
through the wrong end of a telescope,
through the sharpening lens of spite
that made him smaller, the clearer he became.
And she was almost sorry, sorry for them both
because she knew she would never again

give up this clarity. It was easier,
she knew now, to forget his brief
vagrant lapses into care
than to resist ever again the hard
current of their long past
which carried her now up and down
the aisles of the supermarket,
remembering all of the old complaints,
how if it shines, she'd buy it,
how she's never learned to live
within their means—she remembered
all of it and pulled down only
the dullest cheapest canned goods:
generic coffee, oily tuna, all
the frozen dinners she could find
until the cart was heavy
with everything he ever wanted.
And as she pushed it, her dress damp
and cold against her, she could feel
the blood ram though the clogged arteries
and the yellow bruise on her hip
from the angiogram begin to ache
so much that she imagined it was
flashing to the check out girl and
to the boy who lugged her eight bags
to the car that she was old and sick.

Her whole life seemed like one rehearsal
for this long drive home with groceries,
clenching the wheel to keep from fainting,
past none of the famous houses to
her own place, where he was waiting.
What do you want from me, he said,
what? what do you want?
But she wasn't done with him, not yet.

She dragged bag after bag up the stairs
through the living room aswim
in a crazy dream of colors
which only tired her now.
And she was still not done, not even
after she put everything away,
washed every dish, and was so weak
she had to let him help her back to bed.
For later he would wake her saying, honey,
don't you want to watch your show,
your show is on, honey, and she would
roll over, tell him she was
too beat, yes, she would make sure
that this last disappointment
and the regret she gives back in return
will be a final understanding
it has taken them their whole lives
to perfect, a sterling intimacy
that she will never, ever let him tarnish.

Mortmain

This much I know—Mother and
Son are stories you and I
can tell only to ourselves,
and badly. You are in mine,
there in every episode,
back to the dimmest first fore-
tellings, but only to tell
an old story of your own
in which I never appear.

We are trained on each other.
Dinner steams on the range, heat
shimmers between us as you
aim another gift my way—
a can opener this time,
of all things. The small hook reaching
from your fist, you hold it out
like something you'd protect me
with, or from, part dare, part plea,

while everything about you—
your difficulty breathing,
and the sweat-soaked darkened hair
you spent all morning doing—
everything announces, "Look
at the trouble I've gone to
to buy you this. Here take it."
All just to have me say, caught
unawares, "Thanks anyway,"

forgetting, again, this is
exactly what you wanted.
Now you can repeat before
you turn back to the dinner
you won't let me help you make,

"Fine. Someone else will take it."
Now you can wave this refusal
like a wand to conjure with,
as though at its touch the steam,

the trembling heat would flare up,
scoring the dense air between
us with everything you've done
for anyone, the smallest
favor, the least sacrifice,
stray ends, rags of thoughtfulness
no one returns. No one could.
This much I know: I dissolve
in this changeless atmosphere.

This much I have learned to ask:
Who is it you are watching—
fixed there on the high ground of
all your secret grievances?
Who is it, held far below,
unable to approach or leave,
trained to provide you with this
generous unobstructed
constant view that you command?

Astronomy Lesson

The two boys lean out on the railing
of the front porch, looking up.
Behind them they can hear their mother
in one room watching "Name That Tune,"
their father in another watching
a Walter Cronkite Special, the TVs
turned up high and higher till they
each can't hear the other's show.
The older boy is saying that no matter
how many stars you counted there were
always more stars beyond them
and beyond the stars black space
going on forever in all directions,
so that even if you flew up
millions and millions of years
you'd be no closer to the end
of it than they were now
here on the porch on Tuesday night
in the middle of summer.
The younger boy can think somehow
only of his mother's closet,
how he likes to crawl in back
behind the heavy drapery
of shirts, nightgowns and dresses,
into the sheer black where
no matter how close he holds
his hand up to his face
there's no hand ever, no
face to hold it to.

A woman from another street
is calling to her stray cat or dog,
clapping and whistling it in,
and farther away deep in the city

sirens now and again
veer in and out of hearing.

The boys edge closer, shoulder
to shoulder now, sad Ptolemies,
the older looking up, the younger
as he thinks back straight ahead
into the black leaves of the maple
where the street lights flicker
like another watery skein of stars.
"Name That Tune" and Walter Cronkite
struggle like rough water
to rise above each other.
And the woman now comes walking
in a nightgown down the middle
of the street, clapping and
whistling, while the older boy
goes on about what light years
are, and solar winds, black holes,
and how the sun is cooling
and what will happen to
them all when it is cold.